**MARK OESTREICHER
& ADAM MCLANE**

A
PARENT'S
GUIDE

TO UNDERSTANDING

SOCIAL MEDIA

*HELPING YOUR TEENAGER
NAVIGATE LIFE ONLINE*

simply for parents

youthministry.com/TOGETHER

A Parent's Guide to Understanding Social Media
Helping Your Teenager Navigate Life Online

© 2012 Mark Oestreicher and Adam McLane

group.com
simplyyouthministry.com

Credits
Authors: Mark Oestreicher and Adam McLane
Executive Developer: Nadim Najm
Chief Creative Officer: Joani Schultz
Copy Editor: Rob Cunningham
Cover Art and Production: Veronica Preston

Scripture quotations taken from THE HOLY BIBLE, NEW INTERNATIONAL VERSION®, NIV® Copyright © 1973, 1978, 1984, 2011 by Biblica, Inc.™ Used by permission. All rights reserved worldwide.

ISBN 978-0-7644-8463-6

10 9 8 7 6 5 4   20 19 18 17 16 15 14 13

Printed in the United States of America.

CONTENTS

CHAPTER 1: SOCIAL MEDIA IN YOUR HOME

"I don't ever want to see you on Jerry Springer."

That's one of those exasperated phrases I (Adam) find myself saying as a parent. My kids—11, 9, and 1—don't get the reference, but they have grown to understand what it means: *You're making a choice that you might end up regretting.*

If, like me, you're on the front end of parenting teenagers, you, also like me, probably have no idea how adolescence got here so fast. Just when the elementary years started to make sense and I felt confident in those concrete realities, puberty hit like a meteor through the roof.

With adolescence upon us and the realities of college looming, I need to have an end goal in mind for my children that impacts every aspect of my parenting.

When my wife and I sit down to better articulate the relational goal of parenting our children, we settle on a statement that sounds like this: "We want to raise our children to have healthy, happy, and simple adult relationships."

Healthy: We want to foster in them a hunger for healthy relationships. Friendships based on love, respect, and mutuality. Friendships that go deep spiritually and challenge them to continue growing in their faith in Christ.

Happy: We know too many people who are made miserable by their relationships. We believe that Jesus sets us free to live full of joy. God has surrounded us with incredible friendships that bring us happiness, and we want to see that for our children, too.

Simple: Several years ago we realized that our best adult relationships were relatively simple. When we spent time with our best friends, there wasn't the heaviness that we felt around others. We want our kids to grow up in the knowledge that their best relationships don't have to be complicated by backstabbing, sarcasm, cutting remarks, drama, and gossip.

The View From (Almost) the Other End

Marko here. I'm in a different life stage than Adam. My two kids are 18 and 14 (actually, they're almost 19 and 15). In a very real sense, my children include one adult and one teenager. By the time this book releases, my daughter, Liesl, will be living in Europe or India (she's going to both) for a nine-month experience of volunteering and embracing adulthood prior to college.

So my perspective is close to some of yours, those who *already have* teenagers.

My views of parenting teenagers are very similar to Adam's, but with a nuance of difference born out of the combination of our unique values, opinions, and experiences.

With that in mind, I have no intention of disagreeing with Adam's relational goal of parenting above. But I'll add a dimension, as I have been asking this question quite a bit myself in the last couple of years. My thinking is that the goal of parenting a teenager is independence. In other words, I'm more interested in raising adults. Sure, we're not ultimately made for independence; God made us in his own image, wired for interdependence. But the dependence children have on their parents *needs* to shift during and after the teen years, with young adults both moving into interdependence with other people *and* their parents. So I'm sticking with *independence* as a goal for parenting teenagers: My kids have to experience healthy independence from me (and my wife) before they can choose another alternative.

And that goal has massive implications for the subject of this book: social media and parenting teenagers.

Before we go on, we should also tell you that the two of us—Adam and Marko—are lifelong church youth workers, with more than 45 years of experience between us. We've interacted with literally thousands of teenagers and parents about the subjects in this book. Adam's really the social media subject expert of the two of us (he even bought the URLs of each of his three kids' names when they were born, figuring they'd want it one day and it would no longer be available). Oh, and the two of us happen to be business partners these days, running a little organization called The Youth Cartel that trains youth pastors and provides a variety of resources.

A Technological Age

Our children are growing up in a time when all of their moments are documented. When we as parents aren't sharing, tagging, or commenting about their lives, their teachers, classmates, relatives, and other people are.

Their births, first steps, potty training, kindergarten nerves, and elementary school days have all been captured and shared in ways our parents never could have imagined. In some ways, we have no idea what it means to be a child today. When I (Adam) fell and skinned my knee, I only had to worry about my mom telling her girlfriends in the break room at work. Now, nearly instantly, we share every success and failure via social media—and friends, family, and even people we don't know are allowed to comment on whatever happens.

When I (Marko) post and tag a graduation photo of my daughter on Facebook®, not only does she see comments from people she's never met (my friends), I also see comments from people I've never met (her friends). It's a weird world.

Relational ideals, the very idea of privacy, and the sense of individuality have been dramatically redefined by technology.

Your kids are likely in a similar position as ours.

SOCIAL MEDIA

Our kids can't remember a time they didn't have broadband, wireless Internet in every room of the house. YouTube® has always been as entertaining as broadcast television. Mom and Dad have always had laptops. Our children have never known a person who shared a telephone with someone else or used a phone that didn't send text messages. They've never had to memorize a phone number—if it isn't already programmed into their phone, they just "look it up." In their lifetime, the news has always scrolled mentions of Facebook, Twitter®, and blog posts.

And so here we are. Navigating the waters of raising teenagers when the moral and philosophical implications of this new technological reality are not yet fully realized.

And unless you live "off the grid" (Ha! It's sort of funny to imagine someone like that picking up this book!), your kids don't really have a choice about whether to engage with a social media-enriched world. Like air, it's everywhere they need to be.

More daunting for us is the reality that our children need our help navigating this emerging world. As Christian parents, we recognize that this isn't just about understanding and using technology correctly. So much of who we are and what we know of others as members of the community and of our church, and what people know about our relationship with Jesus comes from social media. Matthew 28:19 charges us to *"Go and make disciples of all nations,"* but that "going" means something entirely different today than it has for all of human history! Social media has changed the implications of that one phrase in the past 10 years; it's an unprecedented movement that we need to grapple with as parents.

What Exactly Is Social Media?

Let's start with a definition so we're on the same page. (Get it? This is a book, and we're all on the *same page*!) Here's what Wikipedia® says:

"Social media includes web- and mobile-based technologies which are used to turn communication into interactive dialogue among organizations, communities, and individuals."[1]

Did you see what we did there? We used a social media site to define social media itself. Unlike traditional media, social media is democratic in nature, as anyone with access to the Internet can create media.

What we don't want

Less than a decade ago, we'd talk to parents of teenagers and hear things such as, "I don't allow my kids on Myspace®."

As youth pastors, that always put us in an awkward position. It wasn't just that we *suspected* that their kids were already on Myspace; more often than not, we were already connecting with them there.

This isn't 2005, and we rarely hear that sort of boundary comment from parents anymore. Instead, we hear from parents who understand that social media isn't going away; they simply need to know how it fits into their overall parenting goals and objectives.

Instead of building walls of isolation, these parents want to know how their kids can lead lives that honor God, keep them safe, and move them toward wisdom and independence.

The focus of this book, then, isn't a "circle the wagons" mentality. If you want a book to tell you the Internet is evil, you can find that elsewhere. Our goal, instead, is to move from building walls of protection to shaping a focus on understanding social media and earning trust that moves your teenager toward adulthood.

From an adolescent development perspective, building and reinforcing walls of protection for our teenage children—no matter how well intentioned—can become counterproductive. A primary objective of adolescence is to find one's place in the world. This process, called individuation, is unavoidable from a developmental perspective, if a child is to grow into an adult.

One task of individuation is simply this: becoming one's own self. And a major component of that process is the trying on of different selves.

Each of us can look back on our teenage years and remember this process. Perhaps you were like me (Adam) and you spent a season of adolescence wearing Metallica T-shirts and skateboarding. I (Marko) went through a preppy phase, a wannabe punk phase, and even (this is embarrassing) a break dancing phase. (I thank God this phase wasn't posted and tagged on Facebook!) These were a critical part of our adolescent journeys, as we were trying to find our unique identity and place in the world. We didn't become skateboarding metalhead adults, or preppy/

punk/break dancing adults—but trying on those various selves was part of becoming who we are today.

"Individuation does not happen in a vacuum. One needs only look to any seventh grader with whom you have an inside relationship to see the beginnings of what is, at times, seemingly a split personality. He will be a class clown at school, protective older brother in the neighborhood and chief torturer of his little brother at home. He will give a head nod to family in public and fall asleep in a family member's lap on the couch at home, securely hidden from the world."[2]

The same is also true with your teenager when it comes to social media usage. For instance, she may try out creating a personality online that's different from what she displays in your home. Or perhaps he is hyper-Christian on Facebook to inspire his aunts and uncles but a real hellion at home. That's all part of trying on new selves to find who they are. (And the reason this stage is often when parents get gray hair!)

Further, research in the field of adolescent development shows that the more parents try to restrict this process of individuation, the more they often drive their teenagers toward deviance, secrecy, and a lack of communication.

In school, this often exhibits itself when teenagers create new ways to get around rules. Let's say the school has a rule that prohibits non-natural hair colors. Teenagers try to find a new way to express themselves by sticking their toes across the line, by coloring only one shock of hair, or shaving it into a naturally colored but even more distracting style.

This same phenomenon is why it isn't unusual for teenagers to have a Facebook or Twitter account that you're aware of—and then a secret, no-parents-allowed account. (More on this in Chapter 6.)

What we do want

Looking again at the big-picture goal: As Christian parents, we want our kids to grow up to experience more than healthy, happy, and simple adult relationships, don't we?

We know from our own walk with Jesus that *living* as a Christian is about much more than *behaving* like a good Christian. We aim to experience the fullness of life God offers and to live a life that brings others closer to Jesus.

As we journey together, we need a hearty, grace-filled emphasis. We don't want to merely teach our kids what to do and what not to do. Instead, we want them to live all aspects of their lives in a way that has been transformed by the working of the Holy Spirit in their lives—as messy and scary as that is!

Along the way there are things that you'll want to help your child avoid altogether. We want this book to empower you with both understanding and practical skills you can implement right away.

But we'll also be in constant consideration of their adult faith development. We want teenagers to avoid pitfalls, but we *really* want them to grow in wisdom—and their social media usage is now an enormous part of that.

Imagine your child as a college freshman—sitting in a dorm, far from home, and intertwined in an impossible array of newfound relationships. By the time they're sitting in that place, making decisions that will impact the way they view themselves for years to come, it's really too late for rules. They need to have acquired social media wisdom by then.

With that in mind, let's begin preparing them.

CHAPTER 2:
WHAT ARE TEENAGERS
ACTUALLY DOING ONLINE?

Fifteen years ago my wife and I (Adam) lived in a high-rise apartment building in downtown Chicago. Before we moved in, we assumed that living 15 stories above the street would afford us a certain level of privacy. We were newlyweds, and the 800-square-foot apartment seemed like a palace compared to our dorm rooms.

That sense of privacy lasted until the very first night in our new apartment. During a commercial break in *Mad About You*, I dashed to the kitchen to grab a snack. But I only got about halfway there. As I walked by one of our wide-open windows, I stopped dead in my tracks, because I could see directly across the street into our neighbors' living room. Just 100 feet across LaSalle Boulevard sat another couple on another couch watching *Mad About You*! It was shocking how close and clear everything in their apartment was. That's when it dawned on me: They could see into our apartment *just as easily*. Instinctively, I turned off the lights and closed the shades.

Here's the interesting thing. For the next year both my wife and I would catch each other looking out the window. We had to intentionally *not* look out the window. For 10 to 15 seconds we'd just automatically gaze out into other people's apartments before we even realized we were doing it. It was completely innocent, and we never saw anything. Once in a while, we'd look over and see one of our neighbors doing the exact same thing, staring into our window. One thing became clear: Our neighbors' lives were just as boring as ours.

I share this story to affirm that we're all naturally curious. We might have differing senses of propriety, but we all have a bit of a voyeur in us. So it's only natural that you are curious about your child's Internet activity—both out of parental concern, and out of sheer nonjudgmental curiosity. It's not creepy. It's not weird. It's perfectly normal to want to know what they are doing. You knew them before they had private space. More importantly, you want to know if what they are doing is normal or if it something you should be concerned about.

If you have concerns that looking at their online activity might be overstepping your "parental boundaries," infringing on the secrecy your teenager deserves…well, we want to encourage you to let go of those concerns.

That is the purpose of this chapter. We want to share some facts, take away some fear, and help focus on reasonable, big-picture parenting.

Facebook Facts

In October 2012, Facebook announced that its ranks of active users had passed the 1 billion mark. An active user is defined as a person who logs in at least one time per month. Additionally, Facebook now has 600 million mobile users.[3] By contrast, as of October 2012, the United States population was estimated at more than 314 million.[4]

Of the 6.8 billion humans on earth right now more than one in seven has a Facebook account. And according to Nielsen's Social Media Report, 40 percent of all U.S.-based social media activity takes place on a mobile device.[5]

So Facebook is big and it's mobile (duh!).

But what are teenagers actually doing on Facebook? The quick (and perhaps surprising) answer is that teenagers aren't really doing much on Facebook.

According to a study released in 2011 by Pew Internet,[6] 18-to 22-year-olds (the youngest demographic Pew studies) use Facebook in fairly similar ways to other age groups:

- 31 percent update their status at least once per day; females are roughly twice as likely to update their status as males.

- 37 percent comment on someone else's Facebook status at least once per day—again, with females more likely than males to comment on a friend's status.

- 29 percent comment on a picture at least once a day, with females doing that at least twice as often as males.

- 44 percent "like" something at least once on any given day.

- 44 percent send a private message at least once per week.

To summarize: Teenagers (if we can assume fairly similar usage to their young adult older siblings, which, with the extension of adolescence well into the late 20s, is a reasonable assumption) really aren't doing much on Facebook. While 58 percent of all users log on to the site daily, less than half of those users are doing more than looking at things. So chances are pretty good that if you ask your teenager what they are doing online and they say "nothing," they just might be telling the truth. In fact, while Facebook chat is not overwhelmingly popular among any age group, teenagers use it fairly regularly to talk about their daily lives and homework. Most teenagers are actually using Facebook *exactly* like their parents.

Are Teenagers Leaving Facebook?

In winter 2012, The Associated Press reported that teenagers were fleeing Facebook and flocking to Twitter. This was based on a misreading of Pew Internet's July 2011 report that showed an increase in teens with a Twitter account, from 8 percent in 2010 to 16 percent in 2011. Emil Protalinski of ZDnet.com looked deeper into the numbers and discovered that while more teenagers are using Twitter, only 1 percent of teens surveyed were using Twitter as their only social network, whereas 89 percent reported that Facebook was their only social network.

By the time you read this book, things may have shifted (writing a book on technology always provides the opportunity for it to be quickly dated), but for now, Facebook is still the king of online social media. Looping in social media that isn't Web-based, we might say that texting is the king of teenage social media, and Facebook is the queen.

Twitter Facts

Twitter was the first social network to take off among adults and later attract teens. The normal adoption pattern of social media technologies has always been that a service would take off among teens and college-age individuals, and adults would adopt once it became popular. But teens have been very slow to join the site for a variety of reasons (including that it was a site full of adults!).

Much less research has been done on how teenagers are using Twitter, so it's difficult to point to a specific study on how the site is being used. There's a distinction between the two services that's important to point out. Whereas Facebook makes every effort to get account holders to use their real names, and each individual is theoretically limited to a single account, Twitter allows people to create as many accounts as they'd like using self-assigned usernames.

Partially due to this difference in control and expectation, teenagers seem to be utilizing Twitter in a drastically different way than the typical adult. Most teens on Twitter prefer to have a private account that only their friends know about. They follow their friends who also have private accounts to create a closed loop of private communication to essentially use Twitter's SMS feature as a free group texting service. On top of that, students may have several accounts for their various circles of friends. While adults use the mobile application and Web application for accessing the service, when teenagers use Twitter it's almost exclusively via text message.

This has positive and negative implications. On the positive end of the spectrum, it's wise (even if it's unintentional wisdom!) to keep their social media activity private. Public online information (including most Facebook pages) can be used in ways teenagers never intended, often to their detriment (in Chapter 6, we'll talk about how colleges and employers often use Facebook in their application-screening process). So creating a private, unsearchable space for their friends is a good adaptation.

But it's also been our experience that anonymity (even perceived anonymity) can lead teens to say things they wouldn't normally say. A teenager's Twitter feed might start as a closed loop, with only known friends as followers. But things don't stay that way, and the interconnected social web can result in an anonymous tangle of overlapping social spheres. In that anonymity, teenagers reveal things they wouldn't normally reveal and say things about others that would normally never escape their lips.

In 2009 there was a short-lived trend using an anonymous polling tool called Formspring.me. A teenager would create a single question poll, such as "What do you really think of me?" and post it on her Facebook wall. Because it was anonymous, her Facebook friends felt free to write anything, oftentimes things that weren't true whatsoever because they knew their comments couldn't be traced. For a friend answering the question, it felt innocent enough to answer in a sarcastic, even rude fashion. But for a person asking a question they developmentally needed to know, the anonymity was devastating. So much of what we now consider cyberbullying has direct ties to the Formspring debacle.[7]

Text Messaging

Our assumption is that your teenager's cell phone *is* his social network. While Facebook and Twitter may be platforms for her connections, her phone is her primary access point to her friends. And you may have noticed that how he uses his cell phone is probably different from how you use yours.

- The average teenager sends 3,413 text messages per month; 35- to 44-year-olds send an average of 709 texts per month. So while many parents tell us that one justification they have for paying for their child's unlimited texting plan is so that they can stay connected with their teenager, at least 85 percent of a teen's monthly texting is to people who are not a parent.

- 40 percent of teenagers currently use a smartphone, and 49 percent have phones capable of accessing the Internet.

- 62 percent of teenagers have sent a picture using their phone in the past 30 days.

Also interesting to the texting phenomenon is that the more texts a person sends, the less they like talking on their phones. Pew Internet reports, "Heavy text users are much more likely to prefer texting to talking. Some 55% of those who exchange more than 50 messages a day say they would rather get a text than a voice call."[8] Because the average teenager is exchanging more than 100 texts per day, it's safe to say that most teens prefer text versus phone calls (which sure is a change from our stereotype of teenagers spending countless hours talking on the phone).

As you probably already know, a text message is much more likely to be read and responded to than a voice call, Facebook message, or email.

It's All Going Mobile

In the above sections, we've pared social media usage down to the most popular, most studied platforms for the sake of this short book. But that isn't to say that teenagers aren't using or experimenting with other social media platforms.

We are seeing new trends emerge all of the time. For instance, we're hearing from youth workers whose students have begun using Instagram™, a social photo-sharing site owned by Facebook, to the exclusion of Facebook. And, of course, for many teenage guys, online gaming is, functionally, a form of social media.

The bigger trend, and one to close this section, is that all social media (at least as used by teenagers) is increasingly more and more mobile. As the general public, and especially teenagers, acquire mobile Internet devices such as a smartphone or an iPod touch®, we're certain that we'll see this trend continue to grow.

CHAPTER 3: SOCIAL MEDIA'S PSYCHOLOGICAL IMPACT

The bris ceremony dates back to Genesis 17. In it, Jewish families bring their 8-day-old boys to their rabbi for circumcision. While most of us think about this as a minor surgical procedure done in the hospital or doctor's office with modern, localized anesthetics, the Jewish people circumcise their sons as part of a religious ceremony. The boy is presented and welcomed with a blessing, and then a specially trained professional called a mohel carries out the procedure.[9]

As a new parent the first worry that crosses your mind about circumcision is the pain. While there is debate among Jewish scholars about the use of local anesthetic, there is an ancient tradition of a natural anesthetic to ease the baby's pain during the procedure. The secret? Sugar water. A small roll of cloth is placed in the baby's mouth to suck on and the father or another assistant uses an eyedropper to keep the baby sucking on sugar water.

In 2002, the National Institute of Health funded a study to determine what the best pain management tool was for babies undergoing a circumcision procedure. What did they find? The rabbis were right![10] When an infant is exposed to sugar water, the baby's brain releases so much pleasure-causing dopamine that the baby experiences far less pain than with any other local anesthetic.

What does this have to do with the psychological impact of social media in your teenager? Connecting with another person online through social media releases the exact same pleasure-causing chemical, dopamine.

In a May 2012 article published by the Harvard Business Review, David Rock writes, "An overabundance of dopamine—while it feels great, just as sugar does—creates a mental hyperactivity that reduces the capacity for deeper focus."[11] Just like any other stimulant, the more we use Facebook the bigger the hit it takes to get us high. This is what makes Facebook so addictive. We need to "like" and comment and share to keep the dopamine flowing.

The American Academy of Pediatrics published a report in March 2011 to educate physicians about the impact of social media on pediatric patients. Let's use their outline as a blueprint for examining the impact on our kids.[12]

Positive Impacts

Socialization and Communication: While not the same as regularly spending time with family and friends, social media is an excellent place for teenagers to have social connections with non-peers (in addition to peers). They might not want to hang out with their aunt or may rarely see second cousins, but Facebook affords them the ability to connect with their extended family (and others in their extended web of relationships) in ways that might not otherwise be possible.

Likewise, as we'll examine further in Chapter 6, usage of social media sites can make it easier for introverted teenagers to connect with peers, families, and friends. This enhanced connection really can make real-life relationships better. Imagine your son finds out that one of his cousins across the state has an interest in the same television shows and has similar hobbies. That will likely make the Thanksgiving trip something to look forward to, instead of an ordeal worthy of drama, deep sighs, and the perfected art of eye rolling.

Social media isn't just about connecting with friends. It can also be an avenue of creation! Maybe your child is passionate about recycling or the local pet shelter. Your teenager can use social media to create a grassroots fundraising campaign or learn about opportunities to volunteer. Or they can create a video show on YouTube to explore issues they're passionate about, or start a blog on Tumblr to write about how they can help end global poverty (tumblr.com is a free blogging tool popular with teenagers). These can be incredible avenues to communicate with like-minded people and foster their own uniquely individual voice.

Enhanced Learning Opportunities: Taken Out of Content, a work by danah boyd,[13] is a deep look into the many intricacies of teenage social media usage.[14] In it, she examines the fascinating reality that much of what teens are doing online is learning. Socially, a teenager is learning about the complexities of human interaction. He learns that a person can put on one self in person and another entirely different self online, because that person knows his mother follows his Facebook activity.

Educationally, your teenager can use Facebook as a reliable way to get in contact with people from school. While they might not have everyone's phone number in order to call or text a question, they can almost universally find all of their classmates and teachers on Facebook. (Most school districts prohibit teachers and students from being "friends," but many of our friends who teach say they regularly hear from students and parents via the social networking site.)

Accessing Health Information: As parents, we'd like to assume that our kids would come to us when they have a medical question. But we also know that some won't. Research has shown that teenagers regularly use social media sites to access the health information they need.

In fact, with school funding waning across the country, many school districts have cut funding to health education and school nurses. In late 2011, The New York Times reported that some school districts had started using websites, and even texting services, to help answer student questions. One positive impact has been that because of the perceived anonymity, teenagers are more likely to ask the questions they actually have without the risk of embarrassment. The report references an example, saying, "Ms. Cisneros said she liked ICYC [a Denver-area program called "In Case You're Curious"] for its immediacy and confidentiality. 'You can ask a random question about sex and you don't feel it was stupid,' said Ms. Cisneros, now a senior. 'Even if it was [stupid], they can't judge you because they don't know it's you. And it's too gross to ask my parents.'"[15]

Negative Possibilities

Cyberbullying and Online Harassment: We've already talked about the dangers of teenagers using sites anonymously. Yet even when students engage with people they know, they can be quite cruel online.

Nuance and sarcasm are usually easy to spot in face-to-face interactions but can be extremely difficult to pick up online. Another frequent occurrence in the online world of teenagers is a dog-pile phenomenon where one person will begin a joke about a person or an incident, and that person's friends begin adding comments, liking, sharing, and taking it to further and further extremes. This can be especially devastating to the recipient, because he can't distinguish the line between someone poking fun at him in a friendly way, and someone genuinely bullying him.

As with all forms of bullying, we parents need to take the warning signs seriously. If your child tells you she's being picked on, take it seriously. Even if you look at the online thread and don't think it's a big deal, it becomes a big deal when it impacts your child. Facebook, Twitter, Tumblr, and YouTube all have mechanisms for flagging potentially bullying behavior.

Facebook Depression: Pediatricians are now on the lookout for a phenomenon popularly called Facebook Depression (it would probably be more accurate to call it Facebook-Induced Depression). It's defined by prolonged exposure to the site, leading to depression. (The phenomenon can be seen in people who spend lots of time on other social media sites, but it's been most observed among Facebook users.) We opened this chapter with an examination of the dopamine boost we each get when we have a social engagement online. But just like any chemical reaction, there's a point in which we're so stimulated that the amount of stimulation the brain can generate no longer produces a positive feeling.

Facebook Depression is also spurred along by the comparisons users make between their own lives and the perceived lives they see others post online. While they might be aware that most people edit their Facebook updates, comments, and photos so that they're only putting their best face forward, prolonged exposure to the site seems to lessen this cognitive ability. While the experiences they're seeing on Facebook are largely real, teenagers aren't observing the full picture of their friends' and classmates' lives! In Chapter 6 we'll give practical suggestions for Facebook usage that will help minimize the potential of Facebook-Induced Depression.

Influence of Advertising: Did you know that Facebook's open ad platform gives a wide variety of companies the ability to specifically target teenagers? Don't make the assumption that you are seeing the same ads that they are (you're not).

An advertiser can easily specify that they'd like to display their ad only to 13-year-old females who attend your daughter's school and also like basketball. This level of exact targeting allows marketers to tailor a message designed specifically for your child, in a manner that you'd likely never see.

The same is also true on YouTube. If your son has an account and begins thumbing-up or commenting on videos, the site is learning the types of things he likes. So he may watch an adventure-seeking video and leave a comment. Then two days later, he thumbs-up a Kanye West music video. YouTube might begin delivering ads for the new video camera your son didn't know he wanted but will "need" for Christmas!

Likewise, if your children don't log out of Facebook or YouTube, or even Amazon®, those sites will continue to track and learn about your teenager based on the sites that they visit. Take some time to notice this in your own online browsing. Use Google® to research a vacation destination, or add a camera to your wish list on Amazon.com, and then note how long it takes for an ad for that destination or that exact camera to begin appearing in ads. For Facebook and Google, their primary revenue sources come from online advertising. Never underestimate the influence that your teenager's social media use has on what he or she will one day value, request, or purchase.

CHAPTER 4: STUFF TEENAGERS NEED TO UNDERSTAND

At this point in this little book, you might be thinking, "So what? How is all of this helping me better understand social media in relationship to the teenager living in my house?" It's a good and fair question. Now that we've laid the groundwork with facts and trends, let's get practical.

Everything You Post Online Is Public

From time to time, news stories come out highlighting online privacy concerns regarding a social media site. All of those concerns about your privacy go away if you live life under the simple understanding that there is no such thing as Internet privacy; there is only perceived privacy.

In our houses we simplify it to this: *Don't post anything online you don't want your grandma to see.*

It is in a social media site's best interest to honor your requests and make sure those things you've asked to be held private actually remain private. Yet the simple reality is that anything you post or send online creates a digital record that may one day become public. Remember: You're not the *customer* of these services; you're the *product*! They mine all the information you provide and sell it to advertisers. In early September 2012, Google's stock was trading at more than $650 per share, and almost all of that revenue comes from personal information you, the product, provide them to sell to advertisers.

In reality, there is very little difference between what's kept private and what's posted publicly. Think of it like this: Somewhere in each of these sites is a massive spreadsheet. Every horizontal line is an individual account, and each row is a different type of information. There are simple fields such as name, email address, and your password. But the more you scroll to the right, the more rows appear. One field is all of the things you've "liked"; the next is all your comments on posts; the next is the IP address (which provides your location) from the last time you logged in; the next is a list of every ad you've ever clicked on; the next is the personal (theoretically private) messages you've shared with other users—and on it goes.

In actuality, this isn't far from how social media sites manage data. From a programming perspective, the only thing that prevents everyone from seeing every bit of data sites collect about a user is a couple of lines of code in the program. And it's not completely inconceivable that a hacker could one day bypass all of the site's security measures and log directly into the database and publish the massive spreadsheet for all to see. Certainly, this is already what viruses do (and Facebook is loaded with them these days), accessing lists of friends and sending out information posing as you.

Don't think it's possible? The U.S. State Department didn't think it was possible until the hacker group Anonymous began collaborating with The New York Times to publish thousands of records stored in just such a manner.

Unlike your bank, a social media website would not be liable if all of that data suddenly became public. Yes, they would lose the trust of many users, but don't expect Facebook to write a check to 1 billion users as an apology. They'd just try to move on, as LinkedIn® did in June 2012, when millions of user names and passwords were copied from its database and published.[16]

We know plenty of real-life people who thought they had posted something in secret, or commented on something under an assumed name, never thinking those comments or that message would cause so much pain. And what we've found from our interactions with thousands of teenagers is that only an infinitesimal percentage of them have any clue about this reality.

Maybe you should just read this section of this book to or with your teenager. The point isn't scaring them. Remember, our view is that a circle-the-wagons approach isn't helpful. But we want our teenagers to engage social media with wisdom and understanding.

It's far better to assume that anything you post online, any private message you post, or any comment you make anywhere has the potential to one day be public. That way you are never in the position to worry about things.

Everywhere You Go Is Tracked

Some of this is a little technical, but we'll try to break it down so that you can help your kids understand why it matters. The Internet is governed by rules between interconnected computers. These rules are called protocol.

Any device that accesses the Internet is assigned a MAC address[17] by its manufacturer (this has nothing to do with

Mac® computers made by Apple®). Think of the MAC address as your device's business card. Each time a device connects to another Internet-connected device they exchange business cards, and each computer shakes hands and logs that they know one another. Every time that your computer (or Web-enabled phone) connects to a Web server, this exchange is made and an entry is dropped into the log. While you may be able to delete this log from your personal computer, you can't erase the log off of the dozens or hundreds or thousands of other websites your device connects to on any given day.

On top of that, if you have an Internet connection in your home, you likely have a connection that comes into either a DSL or cable modem, and then it goes to a wireless router. That connection is assigned an IP (Internet Protocol) address by your Internet service provider that points directly back to your residence.

The same is true for your mobile phone. If you have a smartphone with an Internet connection, the same tracking abilities are true. Many phones, such as Apple's iPhone® and various versions of the Android™ phone, also allow applications to track your physical location. I (Adam) know this because I've developed applications that do just that.

At any given time I can log in to my account and see where each of the thousands of users of my app are within about 10 feet. Creepy, right?

All that to say: If your teenager has any perception that what he looks at online is for him to know and no one else to find out, he is sadly mistaken. Every keystroke, click of the mouse, search, and photo uploaded is tracked. Each time he creates an account with a website or phone company or mobile carrier, all of this is acknowledged in the contract, so no one is deceiving you. They just happily allow us to live under the perception that we have privacy.

Over the years I (Adam) have been approached by friends who tell me they're having a problem with pornographic ads popping up on their computer. They ask me to come over and remove whatever virus they think is causing the problem. That puts me in a weird spot, because I have to explain to them that the reason they're seeing those types of ads or attracting those types of viruses is because their computer has seen those types of websites. They aren't being marketed to randomly; they're being targeted because those websites recognize the IP address of that home or the MAC address of that device. It's all trackable, and those digital fingerprints will lead back to the device.

So just like your teenager shouldn't post things Grandma shouldn't read, she shouldn't visit websites that she wouldn't want Grandma to know about.

You Can't Delete Anything

Did you know that when you delete something off of your computer, it isn't really completely gone?

What happens most often is that your operating system tells your computer to encrypt and hide that data from you. So while it's no longer visible to you, an expert could piece those things back together. (That's why the police confiscate people's computers when they've allegedly committed a crime!)

The same is true for social media sites. You can go back and delete a comment or unlike something or delete a personal message. But all you've done is hidden it from your view. It still happened, it still exists; now you just created an additional record on the site's server to hide that information from you. If you think back to the spreadsheet concept of your account on a social media site, there's a column for all the things you've deleted.

This is especially important to understand with sites that are searchable by Google. That includes anything posted publicly on Facebook, on a regular Twitter account, anything on Tumblr, or YouTube. Google regularly indexes all of those things. And each time Google crawls a website, it takes a new picture of everything. So let's say that your teenager creates a "secret" blog documenting how much he hates the ninth grade. Then, one day in 11th grade, realizing that hating the ninth grade might make it hard to get into his college of choice, he deletes it. The good news is that it's gone from the current version of the Web. The bad news? A record of that is permanently available through Google, and as a snapshot via web.archive.org.

Employers Look at Social Media Profiles Before Hiring and While You're Employed

It's hard for the average seventh-grader to understand that her Facebook status comments cussing out her ex-best friend for insulting the color of her dress might one day impact her ability to get hired. And sure, that may be an extreme example. But by the time teenagers are in high school, they need to understand that anyone from a mom who may hire them to babysit, to a nonprofit looking at them for a summer internship, could be checking out their social media profiles.

Potential employers will look at anything they can find out about an applicant that comes up in a thorough search of the Internet. They'll look at pictures the person is tagged in, note the relationship status if it's public, and may even find out what that person did the night before the interview. While it's a bit overstated to believe that what you do online in your early teenage years can impact you well into college or a career, it's safe to say that at some point in high school you'll want to teach your children to begin managing their public profiles in a way that reflects how they'd like to be perceived.

According to an article written by Lauren Fisher of The Next Web, 44 percent of employers openly admit that they monitor employees' social media profiles *while they are employed* (and that percentage only includes those who will admit to the practice).[18]

A few years back my wife and I (Adam here) had a regular babysitter who vented about our kids on her blog and on Facebook. Maybe it was a little shallow on our part, but we had an extremely difficult time convincing ourselves to continue hiring her or recommending her to others based purely on the words she used to describe our kids online. It's not that these weren't things that were OK to say or think. But to post them online? That was too far!

Colleges May Screen Social Media Profiles During the Admittance Process

According to a survey conducted by U.S. News and World Report in 2011, 24 percent of colleges say that they review applicants' social media profiles as part of the admittance process (and that percentage seems to be rising quickly).[19]

We both live very close to San Diego State University, one of the largest colleges in the state of California. For years, the university was known as a fallback, party school that students enrolled in when they couldn't get into more prestigious universities. In 2008, the student newspaper ran a front-page story about the impact of losing their status as Playboy magazine's biggest party school.

Around that time, officials decided the school needed a major overhaul to change its image. They increased admission standards academically and started cracking down on late-night frat and sorority parties. The plan worked quickly. As of 2012, San Diego State has dramatically increased its admission standards so that it's become a difficult school to get into, while at the same time fielding the second-highest number of applications in the country. It's safe to assume San Diego State admissions sometimes look at prospective students' social media profiles. And they'd be far less likely to accept a prospective student who was on the bubble academically but had a Facebook profile full of references to the party scene. That may have been consistent with who San Diego State was in 2004, but that isn't who they want to admit as prospective freshmen today.

All of the issues covered in this chapter are important for parents of teenagers to understand. But other than the impact of your own social media usage, your understanding of these issues won't be of any value for your teenager if you don't talk about them. As youth workers, we're well aware of how few parents (even "good Christian parents") have honest conversations with their teenagers about issues beyond schedule and homework. And as a parent of teenagers (Marko here), I know that conversations of this type can quickly devolve into arguments, defensiveness, and feelings of being overly restricted. So use a come-alongside approach with this information. Bring it up as something you're just learning also.

CHAPTER 5: ONLINE PRIVACY AND THE LAW

Both of us have had strange moments when our blogs have momentarily "gone viral."

For me (Marko) it was when I posted a silly collection of weird nativity sets in early December. When I linked to the post on Facebook, it instantly started getting "shared" by hundreds, then thousands of people. Within a couple of days, my blog traffic spiked to well over 100,000 visitors a day, and I had interview requests from online and print news sources in the U.S. and England. Somewhere amid the craziness, I started to get nervous: What if I got sued over one of the images? I scrambled to back-fill my post and clear up potential loopholes, but the exposure—to my family—was out there. All over nativities made of dogs and penguins!

Several years ago my (Adam) personal blog got picked up and quoted in our local newspaper. Suddenly my blog's circle of influence got very local. Until that time I had been liberal about posting pictures of our remodel and sharing lots of details about the comings and goings of my work and travel schedule. (Each week I even posted a rundown of all that I was doing!)

All of that started to change when strangers would stop me while mowing the grass to ask me how my 5-year-old daughter was doing. "We saw on your blog that she has the flu; is there anything we can do?" Sometimes I'd come home from work and see a car parked outside waiting for me to come home, so they could discuss something I'd written or said in a public meeting. Months later, during election season, some of my words were twisted and passed around labor groups in other parts of the state, and I started to get worried. Sure, people in my little town were nice enough. But what would I do if protesters showed up?

That's when it dawned on me that my own Internet usage might actually be endangering my family.

When we talk to parents about their teenagers' Internet habits, one of the main concerns is always personal security. Parents want to make sure their kids aren't sharing so much personal information that they put their safety at risk. In Chapter 4 we addressed some of the information that website owners, marketers, and Internet service providers log about your teenager's activity. All of that has some level of government regulation, and those companies have every reason to keep that information away from people who might use it for illicit purposes.

But what about the information you voluntarily offer online? We need to have a family understanding, an agreement, to protect the family's personal information for the sake of physical safety.

Let's start off by identifying the types of personal information that could lead to personal security risk. Teach your teenagers to think of their profiles as puzzles. You want them to set up their profiles in such a way that their friends can identify them, but without so many details publicly available that a stranger could find them offline.

For instance, a good habit when building a profile that may be public (YouTube or Tumblr) is to use their first name and last initial. While there may only be one high schooler named Jessica Renè Rafael in Des Moines, Iowa, there are probably dozens of Jessica R.'s in the Des Moines public school system. Likewise, it isn't a good idea for your child to post their mobile phone number anywhere online, ever.

All too often we'll see one of our students post as their Facebook status, "I'm bored right now. Somebody text me at xxx-xxx-xxxx." That's just asking for unwanted phone calls and text messages from strangers.

Teach your teenagers to be very careful about posting the physical location of your house. Things like "checking in" at home on Facebook or setting up your home as a place to check in on Foursquare® may seem innocent and playful enough. But for someone with bad intentions, it won't be long before they can connect a teenager checking in at home with a parent's Twitter status at a younger sibling's soccer game.

Also be cautious about mobile photo apps such as Flickr®, iPhoto®, and Instagram, because many smartphones automatically collect geolocation data and broadcast that when you post an image. It's probably fine if it broadcasts a general area, like the name of your community or city. But it's not a great idea if it posts your Flickr picture with a Google pin drop on your backyard. Most smartphones have a setting for controlling location services. We'd recommend taking a few minutes to make sure that the default setting (usually "on") for every phone in your house is turned off. Then, when you want to use a location service for a particular app, you can turn it on. But starting with "off" will help prevent you from accidentally broadcasting your precise location.

Additionally, it's a good idea to teach your kids to be careful who they're telling about gifts and other valuables. While your teenager may want to tell her friends about her new cell phone or laptop she got for Christmas, posting about it online in a public way can make her (and your family) a target for personal property theft.

Lastly, you want to make sure that everyone in your household is on the same page about online privacy. It doesn't do any good to have one child being careful about protecting their online security, if another child, socially connected to their siblings, is sloppy.

COPPA Is Your Friend

You might be pleasantly surprised to learn that the federal government is on your side when it comes to your teenager's personal information. The Children's Online Privacy Protection Act (COPPA) is modern and actively enforced by the Federal Trade Commission; it's specifically geared at protecting personal information of children, but it also has far-reaching impact for all social media sites.

COPPA prevents the collection of personally identifiable information of any child under the age of 13. COPPA defines this as:

> Applies to "identifiable information about a child that is collected online, such as full name, home address, email address, telephone number or any other information which would allow someone to identify or contact the child. The Act and Rule also cover other types of information—for example, hobbies, interests and information collected through cookies or other types of tracking mechanisms—when they are tied to individually identifiable information."[20]

The FTC has even extended the reach of this law to any company that does business in the United States. This prevents companies from incorporating overseas just to get around these laws. The FTC has successfully fined many companies for breaking these rules, which has put the entire online industry on high alert. For example, in 2006 UMG Recordings was fined $400,000 by the Federal Trade Commission for collecting, without parental permission, personal information of children under the age of 13 who were fans of rapper Lil' Romeo.[21]

How does this relate to parents of teenagers?

First of all, COPPA is a tool designed to help you. Even though it only applies for children under the age of 13, if you make yourself familiar with the language and inclusion of this law, you will better understand the types of things your child older than 13 may be sharing online. For instance, it's common knowledge among marketers that teenagers dramatically influence family spending. So as soon as your teenager starts using sites intended for adults, the site will want to collect as much information about her as possible so companies can begin targeting your family. All of the personal information she willingly shares in filling out an online profile can now be collected, bought, sold, and rented to any company worldwide.

Secondly, many parents are caving in and allowing their children younger than 13 to create profiles on social media sites that specifically disallow people under the age of 13 because they're not compliant with COPPA. Reading the brief description of personally identifiable information above is like reading the description of everything Facebook asks for when you set up your account! As a middle school youth worker (Marko here), I'm amazed how many of the young teens I work with have Facebook pages—with full knowledge of their parents—prior to 13 years old. I am far from being a social media prude in my parenting, but we didn't allow our children to have a Facebook account until they were 14 (it was a 14th birthday rite of passage in our home).

In November 2011, CNN reported[22] on a study conducted by the University of Illinois at Chicago[23] that not only were there millions of underage children members of Facebook, more often than not, their parents had helped them. Here's what CNN said:

> *"The vast majority (95%) of the parents of 10-year-olds on Facebook were aware when their child signed up for the site, and 78% of those parents helped create the child's account, according to the study. For 11- and 12-year-olds, the percentages of parental knowledge and involvement were slightly lower.*

> *"Although 89% of the parents surveyed believe there should be a minimum age for Facebook, 78% believe there are circumstances that make it OK for their child to sign up for an online service even if he or she does not meet the site's minimum age requirement.*

> *"When asked what these circumstances might be, parents most often cited school-related activities and communicating with other family members."*

The problem with allowing your child younger than 13 to have an account with a social media site is that *it's against the law*, and working around the law is lying. It's not that these sites are picking an arbitrary no-fun line; they're trying to comply with a federal law aimed at protecting your children.

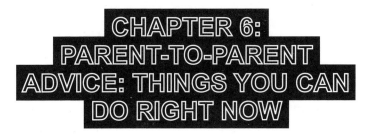

Time for some practical advice. For some of you, this is the chapter you've been waiting for! But these "try this now" ideas all build on the understanding we hope you've gained in the previous chapters.

Remember: Your context is unique. We don't know you, and we don't know your teenager. It's your role as a parent to discern the modification and application of the following suggestions. Don't forget the end game: As parents of teenagers, we are trying to raise adults. We're more interested in wisdom than compliance, more interested in responsibility than high walls of protection, and more interested in healthy parent/teen communication than maintaining a veneer of good appearances.

Where Leads to What

In all our years of working as youth pastors, we've been called into many situations regarding Internet-related difficulties in the home (pornography addiction, Internet addiction, video game addiction, texting and sexting inappropriateness, cyberbullying, and more).

Here's what we know. If family members are using Internet-connected devices in private spaces of your home, it's more likely to eventually lead to private and socially isolating activities online. Conversely, if you create a culture in your home where using the Internet is restricted to public spaces of the home, your kids will be online less, will use the Internet in healthier ways, and will look at less explicit material. In general, the more secretive the practice, the more dangerous the situation. Addiction counselors say it over and over: Secrets keep people sick.

The rule in Adam's house: Practically speaking, no one (including Mom and Dad) is allowed to play video games, work on laptops, or use any other Internet-connected device in a room alone. Even when someone's home alone, that person uses the computers in public spaces, such as the living room, as opposed to in a bedroom.

The rule in Marko's house: Our rules have the same spirit as Adam's, but maybe not the same firm boundaries (maybe because we're lazier parents, or maybe because we're less idealistic, since my kids are older than Adam's are!). Perhaps because of the mix of my kids both being teenagers, my son being good with money, and me having access to hand-me-down laptops, we currently have five computers for the four of us. Each of us has a laptop, and there's a central "family computer" on a desk in the family room. Our general practice is that online surfing, hanging out in social media-land, and other non-homework practices are done in public spaces (often on the family computer). Homework can be done in a bedroom, but with one parent in the loop. And when we went through a period where boundaries had been crossed by our oldest, we firmed up the rules a bit more, to where she wasn't even allowed on her cell phone in her bedroom.

Check-In for Devices at Bedtime

Sleep deprivation is a major problem for teenagers. School starts early, and many kids form bad habits of texting friends or chatting online late into the night. Some friends told us about their easy solution to this problem. This family checks everything in at night. All the phones, laptops, and mobile game systems get plugged in to charge at night in a central location. Now that Mom and Dad are leading this initiative by example, they are happy to report this has done wonders for their love life as well!

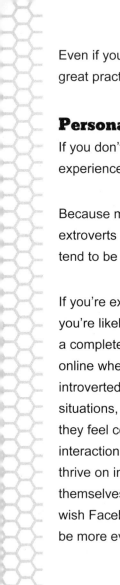

Even if you don't use the "central location" idea, it's *such* a great practice to keep cell phones off the nightstand.

Personalities Flip-Flop Online

If you don't understand social media's draw, you're about to experience an aha moment.

Because most of social media is a written endeavor, extroverts tend to be more introverted online and introverts tend to be more extroverted online.

If you're extroverted and you have an introverted teenager, you're likely to consider your kid's interactions online as a complete waste of time. You think, "Why talk to people online when you can talk to people in real life?" Well, introverted people are more naturally shy in real-life social situations, but because they're able to respond online when they feel comfortable, they may be more drawn to social interaction online. Consequently, places like Facebook thrive on introverted people who are witty and can assert themselves quite well, while more extroverted people just wish Facebook were an event-planning tool so they could be more even more social.

All that to say, if you don't "get" social media because you're extroverted, here are a couple of suggestions for staying connected to your teenager's social media usage:

- Once a week or so, cruise through her Facebook status updates and pick something to talk about— not in a confrontational way, more out of curiosity. An example would be, "Why do you think so many people commented on your status?"

- Ask your teenager to share what he's learning about his friends from connecting online. Sometimes a teenager will notice a habit or even an admirable character trait in someone else before he notices it in himself.

Teach Responsibility, Rather Than Relying on Blocking Software

If you are with us on the idea that *"where leads to what,"* then this will be an easy concept to swallow. When I (Adam) am approached by parents about putting Internet filters on their home computers, I actually advise against it. I know too many information technology administrators at schools who don't think that a filter is an effective way to block kids from accessing illicit websites. Chances are good that even the most pious student at your nearest middle school can disable or get around the school's firewall—or at least knows someone who can show them how. As soon as the district installs a new blocker/filter/firewall, the race is on to discover a workaround that will take students where they want to go.

Instead of depending on a tool to monitor your child's Internet behavior, we encourage you to have open conversations about using the Internet responsibly. When my kids (Adam) first started to venture out of kids' game websites and discovered the power of Wikipedia and Google, we initiated the rule that they could always use Google to find something, but they had to ask us first. They'd come to us and say that they wanted to find new games to play. I'd ask my son, "What do you want to search on Google?" and he'd respond that he wanted to search, "Play boy games." Then I'd explain that those search terms might bring up pictures of naked people, so why not search for something more specific, such as "Monster truck games."

Once your child is 16, however, it's a bit unrealistic to expect him to ask you if he's allowed to search Google for "Foundations of the Bill of Rights" for his homework essay.

But here are some almost-without-exception realities the two of us have observed in the thousands of teenagers we've worked with: Even the tightest parental controls on Internet usage don't work. Teenagers will find a way to access what they want to access. I (Marko) have a very conservative adult relative who resisted all cultural pressure (and begging from his four daughters), and refused to even have a computer and Internet access in their home. His daughters were forbidden to have Facebook accounts or even email addresses. So I thought it interesting that his 16-year-old (who was an extremely compliant girl, not exhibiting even the slightest rebellious streak) still found a way to comment on my blog once in a while, or send me a "Hi, Uncle Marko" email from some cryptic email address.

Here's our thinking (and we're sure there are people who would disagree with us on this one): Relying on Internet blocking software is lazy parenting. And it doesn't work. Better to be super engaged, watch for patterns, and teach responsibility.

Ideally, if trust is earned and proved, you'll want to monitor your teenager's Internet and social media usage less and less as they move into the late-teen years. But, of course, you don't start there. Start by keeping a close eye on what they're doing. And as they earn your trust, give them more and more freedom both to explore and to learn how to handle failure.

Freedom Within Boundaries

With my (Marko) kids being 18 and almost 15, we've stumbled through how to apply our general parenting approaches to the world of online engagement. As a youth worker, I am well aware of both the potential pitfalls and the social realities of today's teen world. And I'm an avid social media user myself—so it hardly seems fair to hyper-limit my kids.

Because our parenting practice has mostly been about teaching our kids to take responsibility for themselves, we've had to give them freedoms. Without the freedom to succeed and fail, they can't grow in wisdom. And that's true in all things social media, too.

So in addition to the natural boundaries I've previously mentioned (such as no Facebook account until 14, limited use of devices in private spaces of our home, and open dialogue about privacy, safety, and wisdom), we've set another "rule" in place: Dad (me) gets all your passwords and will occasionally look in. It's one thing to look at my daughter's Facebook page while I'm signed in as myself, but it's a very different experience to sign in as her and poke around. I look at Facebook messages, Internet browsing history, sent and deleted emails, and (this is a biggie) occasionally look through texting records for practices and patterns.

My kids know I do this—it's not a secret. I'll praise them if I'm seeing wisdom. I'll open up dialogue with them if I observe gray-area practices. And I'll restrict or clarify boundaries if my kids have crossed them. These boundaries, and these "checks," have changed over the years, so that I no longer check on my 18-year-old. In fact, I don't require her to give me her passwords—I want her to be an adult, and that means she has to own the responsibility. But just last week I had a conversation with my son about some Facebook private messages that seemed to be at odds with who he wants to be.

Your Teenager's Phone Is a Social Network

If there's one device your kid is probably totally addicted to, it's the cell phone. With the average teenager sending more than 100 text messages per day, the phone really is the access point to social networks. It's a constant companion, and your teenager knows where it is at all times.

In fact, a 2011 study surveyed 16- to 24-year-olds, asking them which media activity they would miss the most. Mobile phones ranked highest, with Internet and TV trailing close behind. In contrast, only 1 percent of adults 55-64 responded that they would miss their cell phones.[24]

As a parent you already know that texting is the fastest and most reliable way to communicate with your teenager. (You are likely the same way!)

We've heard stories of teenagers texting in the shower by putting the phone in a plastic bag to keep it dry. Many teenagers have taught themselves to text blind so that they can text in class without detection. And if you allow them, the last thing they'll do before falling asleep is check their phones, and the first thing they'll do upon waking is—well, you get the idea.

This is absolutely critical for parents to understand about teenagers. Most would rather lose access to the family car before losing access to their phones. We have often heard teenagers say that they'd "rather die than live without a phone." That's not something we often hear them say about other things.

So there's an opportunity here. We know teenagers need to experience meaningful responsibility as part of their journey to adulthood. And how they use their mobile phones is a fantastic arena in which to learn responsibility, since teenagers care so passionately about access to their phones. Think carefully about how you can give certain freedoms, in the context of dialogue and boundaries. Then actively follow up, observing if the responsibilities and freedoms are being utilized with wisdom or recklessness. If wisdom is in play, widen the boundaries (giving more responsibility and freedom). If recklessness is in play, clarify the boundaries, or pull them in a bit tighter.

And remember, in Chapter 4 we suggested checking in all phones and devices in the kitchen (or some central location) so everyone can get a good night's sleep. This might feel like a steep hill to climb if your teenager has already been living with his phone next to his bed for three years. But we know teenagers, and we know the impact of sleep deprivation, and we feel really strongly about this suggestion (so much so that we'll state that *if you only apply one single, practical idea from this book, we would prefer it be this one*). Help your teenager understand that while her phone might be her social network, she controls the phone—the phone doesn't control her.

Engaging Your Teenager Online

Because one of the biggest and most important challenges in parenting teenagers is keeping open lines of communication, it's wise to be intentional and proactive about connecting with them anywhere and everywhere. Of course, it's natural for your teenage son to be a little hesitant about his parents invading his social space (just like he would be if you decided it would be fun to double-date with him to the school dance!). So be upfront and honest that you'll be Mom or Dad on Facebook (and not some creepy "friend").

Be sensitive about both engagement and not overstepping ("Hi sweetie! I washed your bed sheets today, even though you said I should leave them alone."). Right: You probably didn't want your parents involved in everything you did in high school either. That's why it's important to know that there is a difference between having access and being pesky. For instance, you might want to ask if it's OK if you like, comment, or share pictures your daughter posts on Facebook. Or if you notice that your son is doing something online that you don't like, make sure you talk to him directly about it rather than leaving an embarrassing admonishment online for all of his friends to see.

Be aware of your own activity as well. Remember: They're watching you, too!

The Underlying Issue Isn't New...

Today it's texting, Facebook, YouTube, Twitter, and Tumblr. Tomorrow it'll be something else. Parents are typically overwhelmed with so many other things to manage that the thought of having yet another technology to figure out can be daunting. We've talked to many parents who have just chosen to ignore their teenager's online activities because it's something they simply don't understand, and they don't have the time or interest to bother with it.

Let's not make that mistake. Instead, let's frame all of social media into something all parents already understand. Social media is just an online version of the complex social relationships you—as an adult—have already learned how to navigate.

Part of becoming an adult is learning how to act around various groups of people, and in various contexts. Chances are good you've learned how to appropriately address relationships at work and how that's different from church. You might still find conflict with friends awkward, but you've dealt with it plenty of times. So while you may not be as comfortable (or fast!) as your teenager when it comes to Facebook or text messages, you know relationships. You know conflict. You know about hurt feelings, and the politics of some friendships, and even—if you think back some years—about what relationships feel like as a teenager.

Sometimes it's simply a matter of empathizing with your kids. Can you recall a time when a relationship went sour in junior high, and you thought everyone was going to hate you forever? Sure, you're older now, and you now know the end result wasn't what you expected. But for your seventh-grader, the problem unfolding on Facebook can be just as devastating.

When we were in junior high, no one had cell phones, and the Internet didn't exist yet (we'd barely emerged from caves!). But we did have a complex social structure impacted by the technology of the day. During class I (Adam) would write a note and fold it up to give to my friend who would see my girlfriend in the next class. She'd read the note and write a response that she'd hand to another friend who brought it to my locker. It was archaic, but there were rules and complexities that everyone observed. If you broke a rule, there were negative social consequences. And if you were trustworthy, you got more friends who would trust you with their notes.

So don't get lost in the technology. You're already good at managing the relational aspects of life; it's just the technology that changes.

You Can Do This!

We know that this book has been short and to the point, but also delivered a bit of a fire hose of information. Our hope, as we've stated many times in many ways, is that you've gained understanding about how social media works and that it will inform your overall parenting goals.

The best news for you is that every study about influences in the lives of teenagers reveals that parents have the greatest influence—more than peers, more than "youth culture," and more than the Internet or social media. So while we've pointed to lots of statistics and given lots of advice on technologies you may not fully understand, never forget that God equipped and prepared you for this amazing task of raising his beloved children.

ENDNOTES

1. en.wikipedia.org/wiki/Social_media

2. Amy Jacober, The Adolescent Journey: An Interdisciplinary Approach to Practical Youth Ministry (Downers Grove, IL: InterVarsity Press, 2011), 62 (http://books.google.com/books?id=HpQeDID7-lpg=PA53&ots=rrN8BbDKU_&dq=individuation%20adolescence%20jung&pg=PA62#v=onepage&q=individuation%20adolescence%20jung&f=false)

3. newsroom.fb.com/ImageLibrary/detail.aspx?MediaDetailsID=4227 (accessed October 5, 2012)

4. census.gov/main/www/popclock.html (accessed October 5, 2012)

5. blog.nielsen.com/nielsenwire/social

6. pewinternet.org/Reports/2011/Technology-and-social-networks.aspx

7. usnews.com/opinion/blogs/mary-kate-cary/2010/05/06/Nothing-Good-Can-Come-of-Formspring-Cyber-Bullyings-Newest-Venue

8. pewinternet.org/Reports/2011/Cell-Phone-Texting-2011.aspx

9. en.wikipedia.org/wiki/Mohel

10. ncbi.nlm.nih.gov/pubmed/11904624

11. blogs.hbr.org/cs/2012/05/your_brain_on_facebook.html

12. pediatrics.aappublications.org/content/early/2011/03/28/peds.2011-0054.full.pdf+html

13. The lowercase spelling of danah boyd is how she prefers to have her name used. In fact, she even had her name legally changed to reflect this desire (danah.org/name.html).

14. danah.org/papers/TakenOutOfContext.pdf

15. nytimes.com/2011/12/31/us/sex-education-for-teenagers-online-and-in-texts.html

16. pcworld.com/article/257045/update_linkedin_
    confirms_account_passwords_hacked.html

17. en.wikipedia.org/wiki/MAC_address

18. thenextweb.com/socialmedia/2011/08/17/44-of-
    companies-track-employees-social-media-use-in-
    and-out-of-the-office

19. usnews.com/education/best-colleges/
    articles/2011/10/10/college-admissions-officials-
    turn-to-facebook-to-research-students

20. coppa.org/comply.htm

21. ftc.gov/opa/2004/02/bonziumg.shtm

22. cnn.com/2011/11/01/tech/social-media/underage-
    facebook-parents-study/index.html

23. uic.edu/htbin/cgiwrap/bin/ojs/index.php/fm/article/
    view/3850/3075

24. zdnet.com/blog/feeds/users-would-miss-the-tv-
    more-than-the-internet-report-shows/4723

Check out the NEW
PARENT'S GUIDE website!

Check out all the books in our
PARENT'S *GUIDE* Series!

*A Parent's Guide to Understanding **Teenage Guys***
*A Parent's Guide to Understanding **Teenage Girls***
*A Parent's Guide to Understanding **Sex & Dating***
*A Parent's Guide to Understanding **Teenage Brains***
*A Parent's Guide to Understanding **Social Media***

Visit SimplyYouthMinistry.com to learn more about each of these books!